Unmuted

From Silence to Song, Pain to Poetry, Fear to Freedom

R. White

WWW.TEHOMCENTER.ORG

Unmuted: From Silence to Song, Pain to Poetry, Fear to Freedom
ISBN: 978-1-960326-76-8

Tehom Center Publishing is a 501c3 non-profit imprint of Parson's Porch Books. Tehom Center Publishing celebrates feminist and queer authors, with a commitment that at least half our authors are people of color. Its face and voice is Rev. Dr. Angela Yarber.

Unmuted

Dedication

I dedicate this book to my son, Noah.

Noah inspires me to break harmful generational traumas and patterns in my daily life. He motivates me to remain authentic to myself and to be the best human being I can be — for his and my sake. He also reminds me how incredibly loved I am by him even in the hardest moments of parenthood, and life itself.

Contents

Introduction

"Unmuted: From Silence to Song, Pain to Poetry, Fear to Freedom" offers a poignant journey through the chapters of R. White's life, revealed through raw and unfiltered poetry. Delving into themes of domestic abuse, PTSD, religious apostasy, sexual assault, and motherhood, White fearlessly confronts the darkest corners of her existence. Yet, amidst the shadows, her verses resonate with resilience, gratitude, and unwavering tenacity. Each poem is a testament to the author's personal growth and healing journey, crafted with heartfelt honesty and profound introspection. From the depths of trauma to the heights of empowerment, these verses bear witness to the complexities of human experience.

As you immerse yourself in "Unmuted," White invites you to share in her truth, to empathize, to relate, and to find solace in the shared struggles of everyday life. Through her words, she shines a light on the silent battles fought by women of color, often overlooked and marginalized in society's narrative.

Yet, amidst the pain, there is hope—a beacon of light at the end of the tunnel. These poems serve as a reminder that while scars may mark our past, they do not define our future. Healing is possible, and it begins with acknowledging our traumas and seeking the support we deserve.

These traumas may have scarred our lives, but they certainly do not completely define us. Healing is possible from facing your traumas appropriately, under the supervision of a licensed therapist or psychologist. There is light at the end of the tunnel.

"Unmuted" is more than a collection of poems; it's a testament to the resilience of the human spirit and the power of self-discovery. Dive in, and let the journey begin.

Broken Wings

Trapped in a crimson rusty cage.
You have swallowed the key.
I'm slowly growing in age.
Given up,
I let it be.
I let you be.

Feathers of green, red, yellow
Fallen to the floor.
I am naked with no choice.
A lack of color in me
I no longer sing with this voice.
I let it be.
I let you be.

I'm waiting for the day.
When these broken wings
Find the strength to fly away.
Peaceful, soulful

I'm yearning for that day.
When the wind whispers on my skin
Gently, smoothly
Shall it be?

Discovering myself gradually
In this world, I have been caged from
Locked up, shattered, silenced from
But the key still dangles from a thread.
Like hope that I ferociously dread

Hope remains.
My weakness will be drained.
I will be free.
I'll let it be.

Galaxy

Light or dark
Where divisions are elemental,
Where grouping defines your mark

Clusters of constellations don't intertwine.
For the sake of simplicity and to rhyme

Overlap and dare to be complex.
for the shimmers of the nebula
would not shine without the vex.

Ropes of Maui

The lock jingles against the metal
Heavy and dull
There is no reflection.
I sit here beneath this cold lock.
My hand slides out of the bars.
"The other side feels the same," I wonder.
Yet, it is distinct.

My fingers curl around the metallic bars
My eyes peek through with curiosity
I see rays set behind the surface.
Sunbeams across the cloudy horizon
A harp plays an inviting melody.
Like music notes swarming in waves

My eyes open wider with comfort.
And my hands slide down the bars,
Onto the metal chains and lock
A *sigh* is released with a realization.
My palms return to the sides of my firm thighs.

The golden rays shine a little brighter,
And right into the jail cell
"If only I had a rope,
I would lasso the sun," I thought.
Let it beam closer with its warm rays.

The glitter of hope and survival
Mist bounces off each ray,
And shines through the rusty lock.
I sit here and feel the heat radiate my hair.
What was once dark,
Transforms into ruby red.

My eyes gently blink as the light shines through.
And at that moment,
I became willing.

Foggy Afternoon

Water drops are on each grass
They slide down
One by one
The mist and fog crashes
Cotton candy clouds that weigh a ton

A mother holds onto her baby
As her baby *pitter-patter, babble dabbles*
They swing back and forth where it's shady
The baby is amazed.
The baby is aghast.

The mother comforts her little one.
Swinging under a tree in Belfast
Fog blurs the horizon
The hair on the baby's head begins to curl
Each curl swirls like a ribbon.

Loving fog, cloudy pearls
They say the fog makes it grainy.
As the stems grow longer and veiny
Not for the mother and her baby
The fog simply allows for
More time to be tender and lazy

Worthy

By design,
We are told that
Our worth is defined by others
As an act of rebellion,
I dare you to seek your worth
Within you.

No one can attest to your growth.
From the vast chapters of your life
You are not the same person as you were yesterday.
Your development is a testimony of your worth.

They will tell all sorts of things about you,
Be it true or false.
But only you could know your value.
You are completely worthy.

Love

We can be as logical.
As one can be.
But love is illogical,
It is magical.
You could guard your heart.
Yet be so blinded by infatuation.
Love is what makes us alive and high.

Trick-or-treat, trick-or-treat.
The heart skips a beat.
It often comes with cold, sharp thorns.
Undeniable
Inescapable
Uncomfortable,
Yet, it can be your home.

Love will make you question your world.
It makes you weak,
Then strong,
Then weak again
What a funny thing, that love
Yet there is no meaning to life.
Without it

High alert
Always turned on
Skeptical and untrusting
She is trying her best,
The best to relax and rest.

Her mind is running a marathon.
A race with no winning reward
Situation A, situation B, situation C
Muscles are tense.
Body stiffens.
But her mind? Her mind is flying.

Double lock, no, triple lock
Sudden movements and sounds.
Cause her mind to pace backward.
Like a black hole
She takes one step forward,
And three steps back

"Relax, deep breaths,
Try your counting method."
1, 2, 3, 4, 5…
"Good. Now, tell me what do you see around you?
What are you thankful for?"

Fetal Position

That will solve these racing thoughts.
Red handprints on her thin neck
Her collar bones are freshly scabbed.
"Wake up! Wake up!
It's only a dream. You're OK."

Is she being dramatic?
This is dramatic.
"This is normal for what you have been through.
You're handling yourself very well,
Recognize that. I'm proud of you."
She looks away with a reserved smile.
"Proud of me? I'm merely surviving."

Insomnia or night terrors
These are her choices.
She is fortunate if she wakes up.
And forgets her dreams.

Instead, she wakes up to being on a ledge.
She is hanging off the cliff with one hand.
Her fingers are painfully holding onto the ledge.
Her stomach drops with fear.
One looks down into the dark abyss.

If she lets go,
She may never return.
Fetal position
Hopeless, cold, afraid
A familiar touch causes her to quiver.
A scent leads to a fainting body.
Sounds turn into rage and tears.
There are, however, a few good days.
She is surviving.
Perhaps overpowering it

Respect Thy Skin

Nourish thy skin,
Nourish thy body.
More importantly,
Nourish thy baby.
This creation of love and life
Is a miracle, a new chapter.

With nourishment comes growth
Thy skin will grow and stretch.
As it houses this new life

"Motherhood is a beautiful blessing,"
These are the words mothers hear.
Yet postpartum creeps in
The belly lies heavy and vacant.
Over their hip bones

Stripes form a collage all over
What was once solid,
Becomes soft to the touch.
Pudgy, discolored, loose.

"But you carried life!
Give yourself a break!"
More words are directed at them.

Mourning your physical self
Your mental state
Unable to identify your reflection.
In the mirror

"Respect thy skin,
This is a blessing,
Don't complain."
They respect it.
They even embrace it.
Yet they still feel.

Nurture

Nature versus nurture
A stream of sweet milk flows
Heavy breasts carry nourishment.
To feed the innocent little one
 Sometimes it is painful,
Sometimes it is simple.

The moon is full.
Baby wakes for comfort
Baby wakes for fuel
Baby wakes because
She is longing for your embrace.

Nurturing is more than milk.
It is skin-deep.
Just like the skin-to-skin touch
The time between
A mother and a young child
Is short-lived.

So, nourish your baby.
Spend your hours with her.
Make her smile.
Even in the middle of the night

It's nature versus nurture.
She will trust reaching out to you.
Throughout her life.

Smooth or Edgy

She wanted to have a smooth journey.
Like those ads you see of dark chocolate
Dripping, delicious, dizzy delight
Those who can go and return home without fear.
Those who aim to only do their best, no more or less.

She aimed for that, to live authentically.
Brutally honest, fully alive, with such intention
Smooth like the Kingdom's valley
With rivers of warm milk and sweet honey
Smooth like velvet cloth being sold at the fabric shop.

But it wasn't that easy for her.
Her life would be dominated by unwritten rules.
When to wake up, eat, sleep, dream.
What time to go to school, go straight home,
And to never speak a word of her home life to anyone

She was just a child, trying her best.
But her "best" wasn't enough.
Her path was an edgy, rocky terrain.
Where one wrong step could pull you down
Deep into the hidden cave
Depression and danger
There were no warning signs.

She just had to know,
By being careful, calculated, and in fear.
She can see the other smooth paved paths.
Amongst the tall leafy trees
All she needs to do is leap over quietly.

But the path she was dealt with was thorny.
"It isn't that simple," is what she was told.
"However, if you follow the rough path,
You will be good."

Time passed and her legs and arms were sliced up.
From walking and crawling up the edgy path
Her hair curled into stressful dreads.
Her skin was darkened from the merciless sun.
And her eyes were puffy and wet.

Tears dropped with each step onto the terrain she was dealing with.
She glanced at the children smiling with glee.
Over on the smooth paved paths
And wondered to herself,
"Why them, and not me?"

Child of the Wild

Bare feet on the crisp grass
I feel the Earth calling my name.
She whispers, *"You're home."*

My fingers pull the stems off the ground.
The scent of freshness lingers.
The sun shines beneath my smile,
And fills my body with warmth.

A breeze storms on by
The leaves dance in the air
Dirt seeps in between my toes
Muddied feet from skipping in the woods.

Splashing brisk water onto my face
I am the Child of the Wild
I am home.

The Belief System

We have a belief system.
That is hard to believe in
We have a belief system.
That veils injustices and trauma

Sometimes it works.
Other times it fails.
But we allow it to fail.
Failure is easier to believe.
Then the voice and tears of a victim

We call them survivors,
Yet we continue to fail them.
This belief system is meant to be
Noble, full of justice, and pride

You see, nobody wanted to hear about
The injustices and corruption
It dampens their day.
What an emotional inconvenience

So, we uphold a belief system.
That makes it too easy to not.
Believe in or care for the voices that shake,
The bodies that quiver,
And the tears that stream down their faces like rivers

Healer

Dark, rainy nights set the mood.
To take a lavender bath, no foam or bubbles are necessary.
But some Epsom salt to soothe sore muscles,
And to relax a mind that has been running all day.

Stepping out of the tub, naked and drenched
Looking into the mirror and feeling disassociated
Wondering if these olive and indigo bruises,
And puffy eyes, heavy from crying for days ends.
Are even worth it.

Hair is doused in lavender-scented water.
Softly towel dried.
You repeat words that have been thrown at you.
And start to meditate on whether they're true.
Or even, if you know what the truth is about you.

We need a Healer on nights like these.
Nights when your face is immersed in the pillows.
Tears flowed down your eyes, one after another.
A busy highway of tears with nowhere to go,
Sliding off your cheek, to your jaw, and *splash*
Gone, onto the next surface.

You hug your pillow so tight,
to resemble the loving embrace
You wish you received.
Oh, younger you.
You're praying for some healing tonight.

You're down on your knees and praying for hope,
A brighter future, an escape from this brutal reality
That you keep as a dense secret
Is it possible? Is there a Healer out there?

Does He hear your cries? Does He see the truth?

Does He believe you?
Can He Heal you from within?
Will there be a night,
When can you sleep without fear and judgment?
Healer, are you out there?
Is there a purpose to this suffering?
Will this all mean something deeper,
something bigger to me when I'm older?

"A bigger purpose"
"Think outside the box"
"The bigger picture"
Is this what all these tears and pain will garner?
How I hope so, Healer
"It has to be", I thought to myself.

I need to pull through.
Gather whatever courage and strength.
That's left in my body and mind.
And create a plan to truly live with purpose.

Free

The cloak falls to the ground.
The world catches a glimpse of her hair.
She pulls a strand of her hair behind her right ear.
A gust reaches unfamiliar territory.
Her skin gets goosebumps from the wind.

Apprehension but free
She looks down at the rugged cloth,
and wonders why she feels vulnerable.
Yet she felt her face lit up with joy.

She takes a few steps forward.
Leaving the lifeless cloak behind
She is unapologetically unveiled.
She didn't look back once with regret.

Forgive, but Don't Forget

There's this part of healing oneself that is called forgiveness.
Showing compassion for yourself,
and for those who have wronged you
Forgiveness has been the most difficult part of healing for
me.

See, I built a life escaping what most people would have easily
obeyed,
For the sake of survival
I escaped what has caused many to take their own lives.
I'm no hero, no
Please don't call me that.

I was dealt with the wrong hand by birth.
I had two options which became clearer to me as I grew
older.
Thankfully gained new perspectives
"Accept how you're living."
Or "run away and create a life for you,
Maybe a life for future children to never bear witness.
to what you experienced"

Through all the hurdles,
Forgiveness was the most painful part of all.
It takes immense self-reflection and gallantry.
To forgive yourself and others who may have wronged you.
It takes work.

I'm at a place now where I have forgiven myself.
I was a child, or I was drunk, or I was inexperienced.
I was wronged, not the other way around.
And I forgive myself for trying the best that I could,
With the survival mechanisms I knew at the time
I deserved better.

I forgive those who have hurt me inside out,

Who have taken advantage of my drunken state,
People who have beat me down so badly, I would miss
school.
I forgive because as much as I hate and loathe those people,
I now understand they were using their survival mechanisms.
It may not make sense to me,
as my life choices may not make sense to others
And their choices may have been criminal in the eyes of the
law,
But I can empathize that they're most likely broken people.
With no healthy coping mechanisms

We may all be broken people.
We all come with some type of baggage.
Some have heavier loads than others.
Yet, I chose to grow.
And those who have harmed me chose to stay in their
traumas.

I have forgiven them.
They probably had their fair share of mommy or daddy
issues,
Or "weren't thinking", or "forgot it ever happened."
Whatever excuse to prevent the seed from blooming,
And taking ownership of their pathetic, selfish actions

But don't you dare confuse forgiveness with forgetting?
Or willingly accepting toxicity back
My life is one and far too short.
To invite broken people who refuse to grow and heal back in
I need to do what is right for me, and my child.
And surround us with love and acceptance,
Not hide and silently ignore traumas in the name of
"Keeping the peace"

Forgiveness comes from both sides.
I've done my part.
But I will never forget.

Biography

R. White's journey began amidst the hustle and bustle of New York City, where she spent her formative years. As she transitioned into adulthood, she embarked on a dynamic path that led her across the diverse landscapes of the Empire State, finally finding solace and inspiration in the scenic beauty of Upstate New York.

In a remarkable testament to her determination and drive, R. pursued her Master's in Business Administration (MBA) from Utica University, a journey that coincided with the anticipation of her first child. Balancing the demands of academia and impending motherhood, she exemplified resilience and tenacity, setting the stage for her future endeavors.

Currently, R. channels her expertise and passion as a private consultant for the federal government. She also leverages her skills to empower disadvantaged U.S.-based small businesses and nonprofits through her newly owned consultancy. She has also proudly served in the U.S. Navy Reserves, embodying the spirit of service and commitment.

At the heart of her active life despite the abuse and control she faced growing up is her role as a devoted wife and mother. Amidst her myriad responsibilities, R. finds moments of joy and rejuvenation in the simple pleasures of reading, writing, and exploring the great outdoors with her family. Whether she's immersing herself in a new adventure or tending to her garden, R. embraces life with unbridled enthusiasm and curiosity, something she thought would have never been possible before her PTSD diagnosis and ongoing treatment.

From a young age, R. has been captivated by the power of words, finding solace and self-expression through journaling and poetry. With "Unmuted: From Silence to Song, Pain to Poetry, Fear to Freedom" as her debut work, she unveils a glimpse into her soul, inviting readers to join her on a journey of healing, resilience, and self-discovery. As she looks to the future, R. dreams of sharing more of her stories with the world.

Milton Keynes UK
Ingram Content Group UK Ltd.
UKHW020129070524
442290UK00014BC/622

9 781960 326768